THE
ART
of
THE
ROYAL
BALLET

Published by
THE WORLD PUBLISHING COMPANY
2231 West 110th Street, Cleveland 2, Ohio
Library of Congress Number 65-15118
Stock Number A3020

First published in Great Britain
by GEORGE G. HARRAP & CO. LTD

All rights reserved.   No part of this book may be
reproduced in any form without written permission
from the publishers, except for brief passages
included in a review appearing in a newspaper or magazine.

Composed and printed in the Netherlands
by L. Van Leer and Co. N.V.
Copyright © 1967 by Keith Money

BOOK DESIGNED BY KEITH MONEY

FRONT ENDPAPER
Svetlana Beriosova and Donald MacLeary in
the new production of *Swan Lake,* (Act II)

BACK ENDPAPER
Nadia Nerina and David Blair in the same Act

OVERLEAF
Merle Park at a rehearsal of
Birthday Offering

Margot Fonteyn
prima
ballerina
assoluta
as Marguerite

The Art of The Royal Ballet

SEEN BY

Keith Money

THE WORLD PUBLISHING COMPANY

ACKNOWLEDGEMENTS

I should like to express my thanks to Dame Margot Fonteyn de Arias for her help and co-operation in Athens and Nice; to the Staff of the Royal Ballet Company, most particularly John Field, who allowed me endless facilities at a time when the whole project seemed thoroughly daunting; to those certain dancers who gave me friendly encouragement during my many despairing moments; and to Karl Ritter, whose darkroom magic retrieved countless shots which came under the category of 'impossibilities.' All these people made this book possible. The drawings on pages, 10, 11, 12, 13 and 25 are now in the possession of Sir Frederick Ashton and are reproduced with his kind permission.

K.M.

Ushers on the stage of
the Royal Opera House
talking with Carole Needham

Preface

On the day I was born, Margot Fonteyn was appearing as a rabbit in the first performance at Sadler's Wells of *Uncle Remus*. Thus, I cannot claim to be one of those people lucky enough to have viewed the mounting glory of British Ballet from its youthful days in the early 1930's, belonging as I do to the newer generation trapped by its spell. I am only happy that I discovered it when I did, though I had to travel 12,000 miles for my first sight of Fonteyn and the start of my regular pilgrimage to Covent Garden.

As a very small child in New Zealand, I had been taken to performances of Colonel de Basil's Ballet, but I cannot really remember them, and I was nearly six years old before 'the dance' suddenly claimed my attention. The scene was the top-floor tea-rooms of Milne & Choyce Ltd, in Auckland. (For those who know Fortnum & Mason's restaurant in London, the setting is remarkably similar.) Beyond the gracefully draped curtains of the elaborate windows the sky was clear and blue, but for possibly the first time in my life I was not fidgeting to be out under it; I was enthralled by something going on at the far end of the room. On a tiny curtained stage no bigger than the puppet-master's booth in *Petrushka*, a young girl in a tutu was dancing while a lady played the piano. It was the prettiest sight I had ever seen. To this day I can hear my mother's voice saying: 'Do hurry up; you haven't eaten a thing. We can't be here all day!' But at that moment the vision had struck her last pose and then darted behind the curtain, dropping, as she disappeared, the rose with which she had been dancing. Shyly, she slipped back through the curtains for a brief moment and retrieved her rose. Everybody clapped politely and the silver teapot-lids went on clanking.

For days I thought about the girl picking up her rose— for some unknown reason it was the simple and graceful final tableau that really fascinated me, perhaps because of its spontaneity. Many years later, at the Royal Opera House in 1958, that same girl was to give a performance of Odette-Odile acclaimed as one of the most memorable portrayals seen for years. That performance remains as indelibly in my mind as does the solo with the rose eighteen years earlier. The ballerina's name was Rowena Jackson. Between my first sight of the young Rowena Jackson in Auckland and my view of her as a senior ballerina in the rich setting of London's Royal Opera House, there were glimpses of her doing stunt dances in performances by the Light Opera Company in Auckland, and much later, the chance to welcome back her sparkling personality and breathtaking technique during the brief excerpts she gave as a touring star of Sadler's Wells.

During those years, my interest in ballet was also kept alive by touring companies of the Ballet Rambert and the Borovansky Ballet, but they were not always successful in overcoming my restlessness for the sunlight and fresh air of 'outside'. As a schoolboy, I was forced to slip away to Saturday matinées if I was to see ballet at all, and I was usually torn between my desire to see some pretty ballerina, and my longing to be out under the sun. It was not until I reached the grey skies of London in 1957 that I was happily reconciled to a systematic pursuit of ballet performances, and it was the newly named Royal Ballet that soon captured my allegiance. It is the work of the Royal Ballet that I have now tried to document during a challenging six months.

I find it a heartbreaking paradox that ballet should be such a complete art and at the same time be so fleeting towards faithful documentation. Certainly films have made continuous moves to this end over the past few years, but there is still an enormous leeway to make up before ballet is recorded in any way that suggests the real magic which great dancers create for us in the living theatre. I find there is a constant challenge to record in some way the emotional qualities of great performances, not always the mere exterior pattern, and therefore—to establish the mood of a particular dance passage—I like often to move in close with my camera. In order to make any sort of aesthetic impression remotely comparable to the work on stage (or for that matter the rigours and tensions in the background) a photographer must work with people who can inspire him and lift him up from those black moods in which he will so frequently find himself. Fortunately, in any company, a handful of dancers stand out from their background by virtue of rare dramatic presence and personality which creates an immediate image—one which survives the desperate limitations of the lurking camera (ever ready to capture the incomplete portion of a full creation) and suggests, even on the printed page, a little of what actually took place. In this respect the Royal Ballet is naturally no exception—indeed it has among its top dancers two or three whose range of dramatic interpretation, welling from some deep inner conviction, would be prized on any stage in the world. As well as these distinct individualists, each ballet company as a *company* has an atmosphere and style of its own, often readily apparent to the casual observer, yet fragmented immediately one is actually plunged into the centre of the company itself.

Bearing in mind the almost hopeless task of trying to snare this elusive thing called atmosphere, I intended originally to use a considerable amount of prose to try and suggest something of the quality I wished to retain, but no matter to what lengths one may strive, the outcome is inconclusive, since the image in that case must be re-created by the reader, and no matter how beautiful or elaborate that resultant image, the accuracy is open to question. But I am left to a greater extent with two media: the camera, which often lies cruelly and seldom does what I expect of it; and the pencil which, to be of real value, would need to be in the hand of a genius. So one fails on all three counts, and the exasperated reader may well be asking at this stage: 'Why waste our time at all?' The answer is simply an honest desire to pay tribute to the work of a group of dedicated people who are producing some of this century's most beautiful art images; a group of people who are part of a continual restoration of an art to England—a country where dancing had previously not been seen indigenously in any quantity since the days of the first Elizabeth. Now, this country ceases to rely on importation of the Dance and has turned the tide with a vengeance, exporting this art in glowing tours across the world.

Even so, the realisation is still forced upon us that for the printed page we can steal only a single, frozen moment from some exquisite phrase of a *pas de deux*. Such an act really comes under the heading of plunder and spoliation. Without movie film we simply cannot suggest fully a particular choreographic style to those who have not seen the full creation; all we can try to do is capture a series of attitudes that contain the hallmark and individuality of the original. Thus, an Ashton *pas de deux*: tenderly emotional with infinite subtleties; or MacMillan's complicated and ingenious structures, endlessly demanding in athletic ability from the artists, but once mastered, again the vessel for boundless sensitivity within that framework—indeed scrupulously tailored towards these ends.

As a recorder, I work solely on instinct, feeling my way into a ballet along with the dancers where I have the chance; but thinking constantly in line and shape, and still having to guard against those hairsbreadth anticipations and delays that make a frozen dance moment aesthetically unacceptable. Ballets start breaking up into long harmonic phrases, each of which may coalesce into only one single photo or scribble with any hint of the mood and quality of the original. I become so selective that I am in danger of masquerading as a judge instead of merely a recorder, with sometimes less than a dozen photos exposed at the conclusion of a ballet. Naturally if I had stuck firmly to this ideal premise there would have been no book. I am made slightly despondent by the fact that although the relevant musical phrase passes unbidden through my mind with each photo that I look at, this, for obvious reasons, cannot happen to a very large proportion of the readers of this book. The photos are obstinately going to remain as photos— alas! Certainly it is in the rehearsal rooms that the greatest inspirations lie. There, the work stands in its barest framework, sometimes brought to life painfully, piece by piece, but sometimes welded together in a flash of inspiration and communication that makes the whole exhausting day seem miraculous.

Wherever possible, I have attempted to suggest a sequence of events with the pictures; tried to convey some idea of rhythm and movement, whether it be the logical flow of the story or merely some rehearsal discussion around a piano. This has meant that I have frequently had to discard photographs which in themselves were artistically attractive, but which bore no great relevance to the matter at hand. Conversely, I have had to include some snapshots of very doubtful technical quality in order to maintain a sequence, but I am quite content that people should notice my lapses with a camera as long as the interludes have some logical development. With the exception of some of the more obvious stage photos, none of the shots was posed, and there are a very large number taken during actual public performances. The spontaneous rehearsal room photographs show, I believe, the real power of the Royal Ballet. What looks good there looks wonderful on stage, and after all, the workshop is the very heart of the matter. The stage is the final showroom. It has been suggested that the Royal Ballet's strict adherence to much of the original choreography in the great classics is an outmoded ideal. However, as ballet is such an ephemeral art, surely we need these few (precious few) touchstones with the history and tradition of the art? Certainly I feel it much more important that there should be no policy which suggests the personal mime in these classical rôles be matching in precise detail by all those dancers who fill them. It is the individualists (one hesitates to call them stylists) that we care for most; they are the people we need, for they are the ones who really keep the classical ballets *alive*. Personally, I enjoy abstract and drily aesthetic ballets on their own terms, but I should hate to see a whole repertory of them; to me the theatre is a place for the striking of responsive sparks between artists and audience, and ballet can be a prime force in this direction.

This then is a book by a 'new boy' – an 'outsider' if you wish, but it is by one who feels strongly for the Royal Ballet and its basic principles; by someone who is grateful for countless evenings of rare pleasure given by a very great company. I am a believer in tradition, particularly the tradition which Dame Ninette de Valois somehow wrought in such an amazingly short space of time. As an onlooker, I can feel proud that the Royal Ballet is something more than just an English ballet company; it is a heritage for the whole Western World to enjoy. I hope this volume may give a fuller view of the artists and the work they are doing within the vast and complicated structure of England's national ballet company.

Keith Money

Marguerite
and
Armand

My first sortie into ballet photography could hardly have been better calculated to test me; it was the second dress rehearsal of *Marguerite and Armand* with Fonteyn and Nureyev. I had already made sketches of much of the work and despaired of capturing any true suggestion of such abundant artistry. On the second day, my camera lay forgotten for some time as I watched the work unfold again in the first run-through of the day. Finally, as Marguerite began her rapturous *pas de deux* with Armand, I made the effort and pulled my mind back to my task; picked up my camera and clicked as Fonteyn tossed her arms and darted across the stage. That picture, which actually appears on page 18, opened my account as a photographer of ballet. My torments and troubles had begun.

Few ballets in history can have had quite as much advance publicity as *Marguerite and Armand*. The new partnership of Fonteyn and Nureyev was taxing critics severely in their search for superlatives, and when it became known that Sir Frederick Ashton was devising for his muse and her partner a new ballet based on the perennial *La Dame aux Camélias*, the public reacted with a simmering of anticipation. Continually fanned by snippets of suitably vague advance publicity, the simmering became a steady boiling of interest which was unduly prolonged when a foot injury sustained by Nureyev put the scheduled opening back three months. By the time the work was ready to take to

Marguerite

"Marguerite
and
Armand"

N.
watching F.
from the
wings

the boards, nothing less than a miraculous revelation would have satisfied the clamouring first-nighters, who probably took their precious tickets out of safe deposits along with their jewellery. The critics were obviously expecting to be carried out of the theatre unconscious with delight by the time of the interval, and judged under these conditions, the production could hardly hope to succeed. It was awarded a pass, but did not graduate with honours. Nothing could detract from the established genius of Fonteyn, revelling in her authority as a great dramatic actress; nor from the magnetic quality of Nureyev—not holding his audience with the usual display of pyrotechnics, but rather by the intensity of feeling he poured into the rôle, so that it balanced perfectly the power of his ballerina. Left to themselves, with Ashton's *pas de deux* work, the principal pair were a rare delight. The pity is that any trimmings had to go with the feast.

The settings, and to a much lesser extent some of the costumes, came in for a degree of criticism, and the Liszt B minor Sonata, which had proved to be immensely poignant and entirely fitting when played by the solo piano at the rehearsals, suddenly emerged with the chilling brashness of 'Sunday afternoon in the park' when the orchestrated version made its startling début at the final dress rehearsal. At this stage, Ashton peremptorily cut a whole dance sequence with six male characters, but even so, these subsidiary characters were fighting a losing battle with their costumes and empty material. As one might have expected, Michael Somes, with the barest of rôles to work in, produced in the figure of Armand's father a character of great strength and solidity which somehow managed to form a balanced triangle with Marguerite and Armand, and it was left to these three to weave their own spell.

Towards the end of 1963 the insipid dance for the other male characters made a reappearance. The shapes of some other sections of the choreography for *Marguerite and Armand* remain obstinately elusive and indeterminate in retrospect, and it is difficult to know whether or not this is purely the result of 'artistry concealing art' on the part of the two principal dancers. Fonteyn and Nureyev certainly create moments of the greatest emotional beauty in this work; they live these characters on an heroic scale and have even heightened what were never less than full-blooded portraits. Her Marguerite has the power to break us, while his Armand is surely his most thoughtfully projected and fully rounded character. On the other hand, Cecil Beaton's backdrop projections still do not seem particularly thoughtful.

Reedi

14

A moment from the first *pas de deux* of *Marguerite and Armand*

After a short Prologue in which the figure of Marguerite is beset by images of her brief life with Armand, the scene changes rapidly and a gay and beautiful Lady of the Camellias is discovered surrounded by her group of admirers. Armand makes his appearance and is immediately captivated by the sight of Marguerite. She has difficulty in concealing her pleasure at his pressing advances; the attraction is obviously mutual.

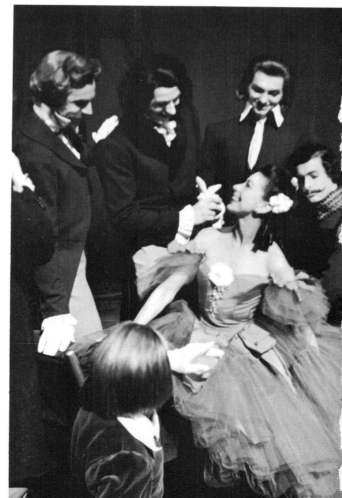

Double exposure on Marguerite's admirers

Before leaving the reception after the first meeting, Marguerite drops a camellia for Armand as a signal of her affection. With an imperious gesture he prevents another guest from picking up the flower, retrieves it himself and, with a triumphant smile, departs. The scene changes to the country. The lovers have a brief spell of carefree happiness (page 9).

21

During a moment when Marguerite is alone, Armand's father arrives and requests that she give up Armand—for Armand's own sake. She ponders on the shattering suggestion, and later breaks down completely, imploring Armand's father to be lenient towards them, but he remains implacable.

There is a brief reunion with Armand before Marguerite slips away heart-broken and returns to her life in the city. Returned to her ageing, ducal protector she is later publicly spurned by an enraged Armand during a violent scene.

These photos were taken at a rehearsal. In this scene Fonteyn should be wearing the white dress after one of the three lightning costume changes required by the ballet

On her death-bed, Marguerite is once more supported by Armand, who has hastened to her side. There are a few feverish, tormented moments left before her end. In the encroaching darkness Armand is finally left alone and despairing with the body of Marguerite

Marguerite's
death

ELEKTRA

Robert Helpmann's ballet is set to a pile-driving score by Malcolm Arnold and is welded together with all the subtlety of a steam-hammer. The first night of this pulsing drama left the audience cheering wildly at the end while critics fought their way from the Stalls to dictate columns of vitriol for the morning papers. For the two principals, Nadia Nerina and David Blair, it was all very different from their work in *La Fille Mal Gardée*. This time there was a blood-red floor beneath Arthur Boyd's powerful and Freudian drawings which reared consumingly above the human figures in this twenty-minute slice of myths for the masses, and for the seemingly nerveless Nerina there were stomach-defying throws through the air, one of them backwards, high across the width of the stage.

There is always one thing to be said for *Elektra*: one cannot easily take one's eyes off it.

ABOVE Aegisthus, lover of Clytemnestra, flaunts himself before her children.
BELOW Aegisthus with Clytemnestra: Derek Rencher and Monica Mason

28

Goaded by the Erinyes, Elektra taunts Orestes with the axe

Elektra, having survived a fairly torrid taunting by the Erinyes ('Avengers of the Dead,' says the programme), is thus presumably coaxed into giving priority to the plan to avenge her father, Agamemnon, slain ten years previously by Clytemnestra and Ægisthus. In true sisterly fashion, Elektra decides that her brother, Orestes, is ideally suited to the task, as is the axe from which she has been loathe to part since the curtain went up. Not unnaturally, Orestes takes a poor view of the suggestion, but after a brief outburst is reduced to foetal postures on the train of Mother's cloak; Mother having been crawling around in the background like a large mantis deprived of dinner. (She wears green snakes around her yellow costume.)

The purple and yellow Erinyes are persistent, never willing to leave Elektra alone for long. The only time she is really out of their clutches is while she is airborne, her arms feathering through the air like a bat on first solo.

This photo shows clearly one of the
hazards of new productions—David Blair
is clearly beginning to get covered with
dye from Nadia Nerina's costume

I must have become rather bemused towards the end of the ballet, for my pictorial documentation gets rather thin at this point. In a nutshell: Orestes, who was obviously a deft hand at chopping the firewood in his youth, is given a chance to prove to his sister that his biceps are still in trim. From a suitable vantage point, Elektra agrees. Rather surprisingly, Ægisthus then holds Clytemnestra steady for the big carve-up, before himself succumbing to a second neat downward slice from the chopper. The bodies jump about like headless chickens. Elektra is reunited with her adored axe; to be explicit— she lies down on the floor stroking the weapon endearingly. Orestes makes no complaint when those two-faced Erinyes arrive to give him osteopathic treatment. They diligently hammer the patient into the ground. Curtain.

Nadia Nerina and Rudolf Nureyev in the scene in which the puppet Petrushka, shut in his box, is visited by the puppet Ballerina. Petrushka becomes over-excited and quickly frightens her away

Despite its undeniable charm and strict authenticity, I have never thought the Royal Ballet's production of *Petrushka* succeeds quite so well as does their revival of *The Firebird*. The production of *Petrushka* has had some magnificent characterisations in the central parts at least, but its novelty has perhaps vanished for the present era. I did feel the genuine spine tingle once—when the snowy sky darkened and the carnival masqueraders appeared, during this very dress rehearsal. But by the opening night the magic seemed to have waned.

Struck down by the Blackamoor,
Petrushka lies dying in a corner of
the fairground at St Petersburg.
The horrified crowd looks on, convinced
that the puppet is flesh and blood

Grant
"Petrushka"

SYLVIA

This vast re-creation in the style of a Second Empire extravaganza is like one of those very elaborate banquets; the solid nourishment is available if only one can dig through the decorations. The whole production has the taste of a 'special treat,' brought out occasionally and then hastily packed away again before everyone becomes over-indulged and bilious, and the management is accused of fostering decadence. Much of *Sylvia* is a genuine treat. The Ironside scenery and costumes are sumptuous in the extreme, dressed with hands that have somehow consistently avoided the heavy touch, and the Ashton choreography has sections in the Grand Manner which are very grand indeed, making wonderful use of the Delibes score. When the production was first presented in the latter half of 1952 it had Margot Fonteyn in the title rôle, and when one has seen the ballet with her, and then without her, one realises just how much of a solid core she lends the work. The three acts, each so different in its demands on the ballerina, tax one's powers of concentration without a magnetic personality to focus upon.

When it was announced that the touring section of the Royal Ballet would open its London season with *Sylvia*, while the larger half of the Company was away on its 1963 American Tour, the decision seemed more like a gesture of defiance than sound policy. No one doubted the team's talents or resourcefulness, but it looked a little like jumping in at the deep end. There was, however, the thought that it would provide a big vehicle for two guest stars during the season; Melissa Hayden was arriving from New York City Ballet, and the Danish dancer, Flemming Flindt, was billed to partner the visiting ballerina. In the interim, there were available two principals, of whom the Company was justifiably proud. Doreen Wells was to prove that the technical demands in the rôle of Sylvia held no terrors for her, and Christopher Gable was to bring great authority to the notoriously paper-thin rôle of Aminta. There were many people who said that the ballet should have been renamed accordingly; it is in fact based on Tasso's *Aminta*, and if some greater stretches of choreography were to be devised for the shepherd, the suggestion would be a perfectly sensible one—except that Fonteyn would doubtless return to destroy the sense of the theory! As it is, the character of Aminta relies too heavily on the interventions of outside agencies during his quest for Sylvia, and spends the whole of Act II in his dressing-room.

The revival of *Sylvia*: Doreen Wells in the name part with Christopher Gable as Aminta

Moment's pause for concentration, before beginning the first run-through of the Act III *pas de deux*

The difficulties of reviving a ballet that
has been out of the repertory for three or
four years are considerable but with
Sylvia there was the added problem that so
many essential advisors were away in America.
However, the indefatigable John Field soon
showed that under his direction, problems
were merely there for the pleasure of their
resolution. He himself was no stranger to the
rôle of Aminta and Michael Somes, before
leaving for America, ran through the
basic moves of the male rôle, although on
paper they looked woefully meagre for a lead
in a full-length ballet! For Sylvia, there
were more scraps of paper, random suggestions,
and a six-page letter from Nadia Nerina. Peter
Clegg, who appeared in the original production,
was on hand to supervise the secondary characters; Bryan Ashbridge's memory was constantly
called upon, and Hilda Gaunt at the piano
obviously remembered as much as anybody.
Meticulously, step by step, the whole puzzle
was fitted together.

One of the biggest tasks was to accomplish
the great *pas de deux* and variations from
Act III, and Wells and Gable spent long hours
perfecting the work under the guidance of
their Director, John Field.

The *pas de deux* unfolds. At this moment Aminta draws the head
of Sylvia gently back towards him, before her arms float out
and propel his hands away ready for support

43

Act I of the ballet concerns the shepherd Aminta stumbling upon the haunt of the dedicated huntress Sylvia (whom he secretly loves) and her female legion. Concealed, he watches them dancing until his presence is discovered. Furious at the intrusion, Sylvia considers killing the shepherd, but when she perceives that love is the cause of his behaviour, scorn and amusement cause her to relent. Contemptuously, she prepares to fire an arrow at a nearby statue of Eros, but the intention horrifies Aminta, who rushes to protect the sacred figure.

Stricken with love by an arrow from Eros, Sylvia
returns to weep over the lifeless body of Aminta

The arrow intended for Eros pierces Aminta through the heart, and he collapses dying. At this moment the statue of the god slowly comes to life and releases an arrow at Sylvia. Sylvia plucks the golden arrow from her breast, and, as yet unaware of the significance of this particular barb, departs with her huntresses. Orion, the robber Khan, has watched the encounter, and he emerges to gloat over the body of the shepherd. Hiding himself again he sees Sylvia return alone, to mourn Aminta. Eros' arrow has had its effect. Seizing his chance, Orion abducts a struggling Sylvia, and makes off towards his grotto palace.

Orion: Bryan Ashbridge

   The body of Aminta is discovered by his companions, whose distress is turned to joy when an old sorcerer brings Aminta back to life by pressing a rose to the bloodless lips. Clues of Sylvia's abduction are discovered and Aminta turns towards the shrine of Eros, whereupon the sorcerer is revealed as the god himself. Eros directs Aminta to seek Sylvia.

   Act II takes place in Orion's grotto. Sylvia is discovered being tempted by costly gifts, which she rejects coldly. (BELOW) Orion is angered at this resistance and calls for wine and food. At first Sylvia refuses to share the robber's cup, but a plan forms in her mind.

Sylvia, using all her feminine wiles, dances enticingly for Orion, meanwhile
continuing to ply her captors with more and more wine. One by one they collapse
in drunken stupor, Sylvia tries unavailingly to find a way out of the grotto.
As a last resort, she prays to Eros.

Pianist Hilda Gaunt
discusses a musical phrase
with Christopher Gable
and notator Faith Worth

Eros does indeed answer Sylvia's
prayers. He appears high above
the roof of the grotto and causes
it to disappear. Sylvia is free.

There is certainly not much
magic about the top photograph
on this page, taken at a stage
rehearsal. The transformation
is effected at the right . . .

LEFT Aminta (Christopher Gable) finally has a chance to display his prowess

BELOW Eros (Gary Sherwood) presents the veiled figure of Sylvia before the mystified Aminta

Act III is nothing but an excuse for a lot of pretty dancing. Aminta, having changed his clothes somewhere, comes upon a festival of Bacchus while still searching for Sylvia. Conveniently, Eros arrives by boat at this moment, complete with Sylvia—also adorned with new raiment, including a heavy veil. This is finally removed by Eros and, to Aminta's patent delight, Sylvia is thus revealed. A mass entertainment begins, but Orion gate-crashes the party with ugly intent. Aminta tries to fight Orion; Eros jumps about rather indecisively, and Sylvia decides that the safest place during the scrimmage is in Diana's temple, standing near by. Orion attempts to violate this sanctuary, but there is a flash of lightning from the temple and the goddess Diana appears and dispatches Orion with yet another arrow. She is furious with Sylvia (BELOW) for the latter's manifestations of love for Aminta, but Eros once more steps into the breach, this time revealing a vision in the clouds which portrays Diana's own past moment of weakness with another mortal shepherd, Endymion. Diana puts a brave face on things and gives the proposed union her blessing. Sylvia and Aminta take part in the final triumphant festivities after making obeisance to Diana and Eros.

LEFT Diana (Elizabeth Anderton) chiding Sylvia (Doreen Wells) for her earthly attachment

The work with *Sylvia* is not yet complete. There is the task of preparing the two guest artists for the principal rôles. Christopher Gable demonstrates his personal interpretation of the rôle of Aminta for Flemming Flindt (ABOVE), while Faith Worth, who has been doing invaluable work making a complete notation of the revival, kicks off her shoes the better to demonstrate a move for Melissa Hayden

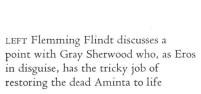

LEFT Flemming Flindt discusses a point with Gray Sherwood who, as Eros in disguise, has the tricky job of restoring the dead Aminta to life

Melissa Hayden
and
Flemming Flindt

De Valois' *Checkmate* is a copy-book example of how a simple theme, coherently realised, can carry all before it—even its own pauses for breath when dramatic moments are allowed to loosen their grip. Its continual survival is a testament to an astute craftswoman.
Sir Arthur Bliss, who composed the galvanic score, was the originator of the idea of Love and Death personified in a Red Knight and a Black Queen pitting their respective powers against each other on a chess-board. There is an awesome inevitability about the Black Queen's chilling triumph over the gallant Red Knight and his enfeebled King.

ABOVE Beryl Grey, one of the great interpretors of the central rôle, in animated discussion of a point with ballet-master Henry Legerton—who from time to time gives us a portrait of the farmer in 'Fille' which is a study to cherish closely.

LEFT John Field recalls one of his own arm-locking positions with Beryl Grey in the ballet, for the benefit of Ian Hamilton. It seems worth recording that *Checkmate* made its first appearance on British television screens as early as 1938.

Beryl Grey
rehearsing
CHECKMATE

Svetlana Beriosova
in her make-up for the
Black Queen in CHECKMATE

Tchernicheva demonstrates for Gable the
hand position which he reproduces—RIGHT

LES SYPHIDES

As is so often the case, one of the most satisfying performances of 1963 was not watched by any section of the Press. *Les Sylphides* was billed for several performances by guest artists during the early summer. One of the guests concerned was the English dancer, Belinda Wright, but this lovely ballerina was to give only one of the performances with Christopher Gable, incandescent young principal of the Company. Gable, who was leading the 'home' team concurrent to the larger section's tour of America, opened the season in London, then flew to New York to re-create his rôle as the young cousin in *The Invitation*, before returning to London and a strenuous season at the Garden. The rehearsals of *Les Sylphides* were once more under the direction of those two great Fokine interpreters—Serge Grigoriev and Lubov Tchernicheva; he having been *régisseur* to the Diaghilev Ballet throughout that company's history, while his wife was ballerina and later also *maîtresse de ballet* for Diaghilev.

The first rehearsal for the Wright-Gable performance had barely begun before it became obvious that inspiration was present. The two artists worked together in the most perfect harmony, paying tireless attention to every detail explained by Tchernicheva and Grigoriev. Together, the four created a spell; Fokine surely smiled somewhere. I do not *remember* taking any photographs on this particular occasion; my activity must have been rather unconscious. The afternoon seemed a brief eternity. When the session was over, Tchernicheva's golden eyes were sparking happily. 'You *will* see the performance?' she enquired of me. Nothing could have kept me away. I resolved to waive the chance to take photographs of the performance itself, and instead sat out front, determined that my concentration should be unbroken. Wise decision! Perhaps inspired by the lyricism of Wright and Gable, as well as the stylish interpretations by Brenda Last and Deirdre O'Conaire, the *corps* produced a complete unity of atmosphere and musicality that other performances of *Les Sylphides* had lacked that season. It was a happy evening; one which left an indelible impression. It was also the Company's 293rd performance of *Les Sylphides* at the Opera House.

'Fair vision, what thoughts, what sounds do you invoke?'

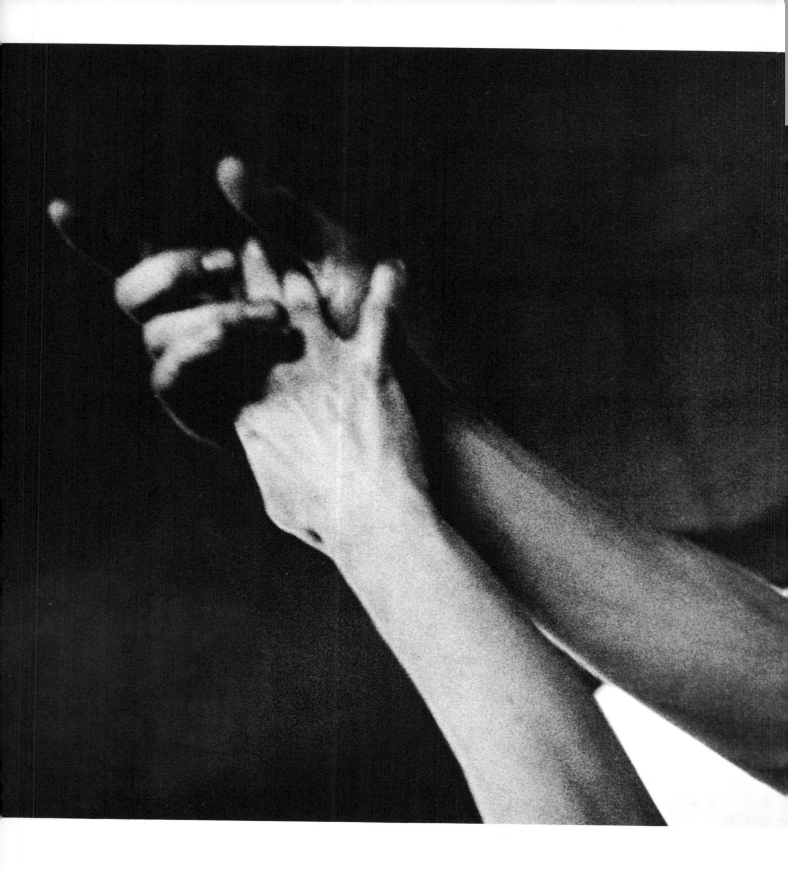

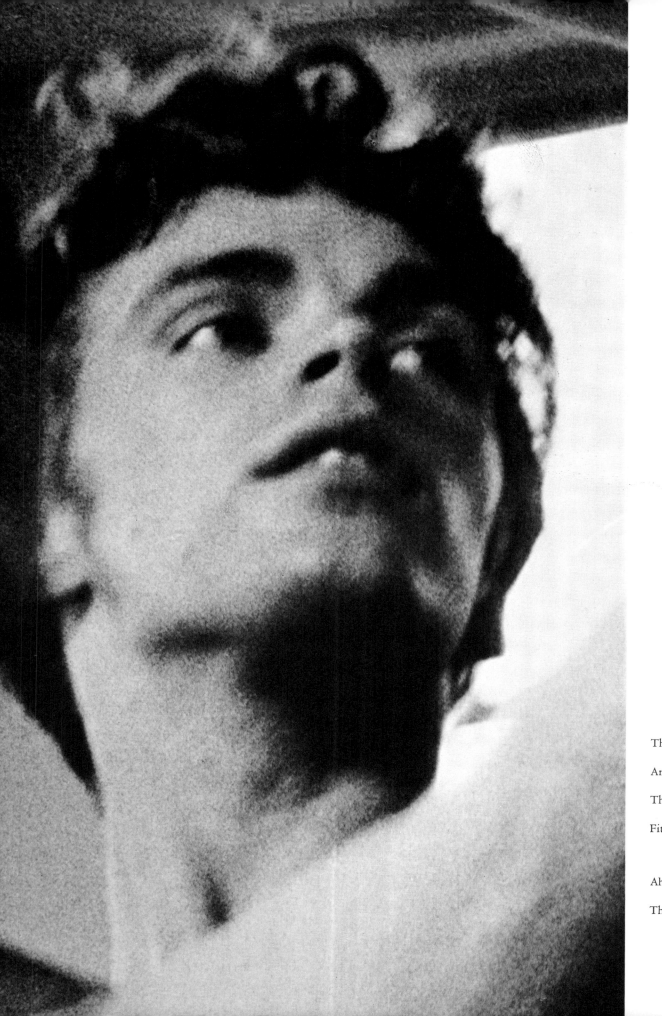

The Poet's eye can reach
      those golden halls,
And view the glory of
      their festivals:
Their ladies fair, that
      in the distance seem
Fit for the silvering of
      a seraph's dream;

. . . .

Ah yes! much more would
      start into his sight—
The revelries and
      mysteries of night:
KEATS

Because of the dynamism of one woman, the Royal
Ballet exists, and exists in its present grandeur.
On the left, 'Madam' makes one of her 7.29 P.M.
visits to the stage, discussing last-minute
points with John Field before returning to her
box for curtain-up. Now that she has relinquished
the reins of Directorship in accordance with her
long-term plan, Ninette de Valois has more time
to devote to teaching young dancers, taking
rehearsals, and making forays to dressing-rooms
with chatty encouragement for dancers who have
pleased her. In fact, she remains as whole-
heartedly occupied as ever. This photo might
serve as a memorial to that incredible Opera
House stage which dancers had to contend with
before the new floor was laid in the autumn of 1963.

Carla Fracci, guest
artist from La Scala,
Milan, coming into
the wings at Covent
Garden

Another pleasing performance of *Les Sylphides* came towards the end of the year, this time with Rudolf Nureyev (ABOVE), Anya Linden, Annette Page and Merle Park in the cast. (LEFT) behind Anya Linden, Serge Grigoriev discusses arm positions with Merle Park

Rehearsal with Mr Massine

The small figure, slightly bent, slightly lame, makes a quiet entrance which at the same time has a very distinct presence about it. The dynamo evidently still charges at full strength. There are exquisitely tailored black trousers, with elastic running under the soft shoes, a loose, finely-woven black wool cardigan, and a white shirt of the finest hand-stitched silk. There is also a hair-net which keeps wisps of hair from straying during demonstrations. The eyes watch with the unblinking absorption of a fierce bird; the hands clap; there are endless halts and repetitions and visits to a small film-projector which throws, from the doorway on to the wall in the passage, a flickering yellow vision of the previous Italian production. It is when the figure stabs at the air, utters a cry: 'Look; you must be this way—so!' and darts to the middle of the room, that the legend really comes alive. The magnetic figure in the centre of the floor then has the plasticity of a youth of twenty, and everyone else looks halt and constricted by comparison.

79

These rehearsals were for the Covent Garden presentation of
Massine's ballet *Le Bal des Voleurs*. The rehearsals had
their own fascination, but the work itself was an unmitigated
disaster. It sank without trace after a handful of
performances and no one even suggested throwing a lifebelt.
From the hopelessly complicated morass in which the gallant
dancers struggled, I remember Betty Anderton's portrait of
the nursemaid with affection. BELOW Lorna Mossford attempts
to elucidate a passage from the tangled plot and counter plot.

Margot Fonteyn

in

SCÈNE D'AMOUR

from Raymonda

Athens, with twilight approaching after a hot, tiring day.
Odd purple clouds edged with gold were drifting above the
shadowed rim of the Herod Atticus Theatre, and two huge
bats looped noiselessly among the arches.

One minute she had been sitting talking; stitching shoes.
'Well, I suppose we'd better start some work,' was the
comment—and she was gone. Two minutes later the newly
robed, remote, absorbed figure drifted past the warm
stonework. Leslie Hurry's diaphanous costume stirred in
the humid air; the whole thing *was Raymonda* . . .

SCÈNE D'AMOUR

in performance   RIGHT

GISELLE
Act II

*Svetlana Beriosova
and
Donald MacLeary*

LEFT   the gift of flowers

Forced by the inexorable Myrtha,
Queen of the Wilis, to dance until he
collapses, Albrecht is sustained by
the spirit of Giselle until dawn when
the Wilis' power is broken

RIGHT Deanne Bergsma, who
brings beauty and elegance to
a number of important roles,
including the relentless Myrtha;
also the Lilac Fairy in *The
Sleeping Beauty* and Berta
in *Ondine*

THE SLEEPING BEAUTY

Svetlana Beriosova

ABOVE Svetlana Beriosova during the *jeté* moment of a glorious *coupé jeté en tournant*—one of the six that occur during Aurora's entrance in the Vision scene. This great essay in classicism being an Everest for ballerinas, it is amazing the line-up of fine Auroras the Royal Ballet *can* display—all with their own qualities. Perhaps no one else gives us the impulsive sixteen-year-old that Fonteyn can produce for us, but her interpretation is one more joy to add to many splendid treats.

Svetlana Beriosova's Aurora is a magnificent creation of flawless dancing in the grand manner. She can take our breath away with the sweep, control, and unfailing single-mindedness and direction that never for a moment wavers from her view of the rôle as a whole.

The Prince holds out a supporting hand which Aurora is about to take, bending her right leg and then rising slowly, straight from point. This ever ready support by the male partner seems a very obvious epitome of so much of 'Beauty.' From the Rose Adagio onwards, any moment's uneasiness in this vital partnering checks the breath of every onlooker. It is choreography by a high-class ringmaster.

More spectacular lifts and fish dives from Svetlana Beriosova and Donald MacLeary—followed by a moment of relative calm as counterpoint

92

Beriosova
as Princess Aurora,
immediately after performance

Curtain call for Svetlana Beriosova and Donald MacLeary after brilliant dancing in a performance which was, happily, glowing and revitalised as a whole. Curtain calls are such an art in themselves; and how does that hilarious pandemonium on stage always manage to sort itself out by the time the curtain parts again on a full call?

THE
SLEEPING
BEAUTY

*Anya Linden
and
Desmond Doyle*

On the left, Ailne
Phillips, Principal
Teacher and a great
and beneficial
influence behind
the scenes,
rehearses Anya
Linden as Aurora

Aurora's entrance for the Rose Adagio.
Quicksilver movements swinging from left to right, with the
arms floating out to match each snap extension. The ballerina
would normally be looking at a point beyond her extended toe,
but Anya Linden is here checking her position in the mirror.

THE
TWO
PIGEONS

Frederick Ashton's *The Two Pigeons* is a bouquet of heart-warming and unashamed Romanticism that made its first appearance in the repertory at a Gala on St Valentine's Day, during a winter season when many people must have been grateful for some form of escapism. Life seemed intolerably serious on the international front, and in the theatre, the kitchen sink was beginning to overflow with drab realism. *Les Deux Pigeons*, as it was known in those days, cocked a snook at all that. Attic studios in Paris became architecturally illogical and overrun not with mice but with hordes of spangled gypsies.

The whole thing was received with delight by its audiences, and rightly so. Its choreography is full of lovely strokes; never overstated, but with an infinite variety of shading in posture and body line capturing the pigeon motif for the principals. The atmosphere of the ballet has in the past suffered more than most from cast changes in the male lead, but no one is likely to forget the exquisitely timed comedy and the moving tenderness between the original pair of lovers—Christopher Gable as the young artist and Lynn Seymour as his delicious attic 'pigeon.' As performed by these two intensely lyrical dancers, the long final *pas de deux*—with the pair of white pigeons joining in—has the fragile beauty of rare porcelain, and its emotional sincerity never fails to reduce people to tears. It *can* be one of the most beautiful and memorable passages in the whole of modern-day ballet.

When the curtain goes up, Pepio is busy at work in his studio, painting a portrait of Gourouli. The model is bored. Each time Pepio turns his back for an instant, she has a fit of the jiffles, squirming and fidgeting in her uncomfortable chair. Pepio even finds her at one moment laboriously inching off the chair, stalking an insect with her foot

Lynn Seymour
and
Christopher Gable

Poor Pepio becomes more and more exasperated.
Trying to take proportions for the portrait,
he finds his model twisting and clowning under
his intent gaze. She cannot sit still; she
bounces about, distracting him from
his work. When he flops down in a chair in
disgust, her boisterous efforts to restore his
good humour are shrugged off

The efforts to get Gourouli to return to her correct pose are never very successful.
Gourouli promises to be good, but invariably spoils the effect by taking up the wrong position

Gourouli's efforts to restore Pepio's sense of humour are wry and funny—for the audience, if not for Pepio. RIGHT She has tried to perch herself on his knee, and instead ended up with a bump on the floor

A group of travelling gypsies, seen passing in the street below, has been invited up to the studio to provide some entertainment. Gourouli, who encouraged Pepio to summon the vagrants, now regrets her action when she sees his spirits so quickly restored by the sight of the beautiful gypsy girl Djali.

Soon there are flashes of feminine temperament and jealousy, with Gourouli desperately striving to outdo the gypsy girl's shoulder waggling and bravura dance steps. Finally, Pepio has to intercede to prevent Gourouli coming to blows with the interloper.

Seymour and Anderton

Gourouli becomes more and more worried as she sees Pepio's increasingly apparent interest in Djali. Gourouli tries to dance with Pepio, but he will not pay her his full attention.

At the end of Act I, Pepio decides he must follow the gypsy girl, leaving Gourouli heart-broken in the studio

108

My documentation of the gypsy encampment scene is here
lacking, but I am concentrating on the changes in rapport
between Gourouli and Pepio. In the final scene of Act II,
Gourouli has sent one of the studio pigeons to seek Pepio
who, in the meanwhile, has been thrown out of the gypsy
encampment and left lying bruised and friendless. The pigeon
flies down to him; he reaches out and the bird flutters to
his hand. Tenderly cradling the creature, Pepio's thoughts
turn repentantly to Gourouli. He drags himself homewards
carrying the pigeon.

Gourouli is alone, waiting. The weary Pepio enters.
Humble and contrite, he shows Gourouli their pigeon; both
pigeon and lover are home again.

Then begins the last ecstatic *pas de deux*, one of the most
exquisite dances ever invented by Frederick Ashton, undescribable
by any words of mine and for the most part beyond the
limitations of the camera.

An
outstanding
ballet
partnership

Christopher Gable
Lynn Seymour

February 14   1961

"Les deux Pigeons"

final

Margot Fonteyn

Utter purity of line creating
a quite remarkable harmony with
the geometry of the room itself

Fonteyn and Nureyev

LE CORSAIRE

Anthony Dowell as Oberon *Antoinette Sibley* as Titania in *Frederick Ashton's* THE DREAM

Premièred April 2, 1964 as part of the Shakespeare quater centenary celebrations

Pas de deux from
FLOWER FESTIVAL
AT GENZANO

A gay, stylish number in which a boy and a girl should be seen to be totally engrossed in each other's activity. The lightness and precise delicacy of the Bournonville choreography needs meticulous study by those not fully versed with the Danish style. The Royal Theatre, Copenhagen, gave Erik Bruhn permission to reproduce both this *pas de deux* and the famous *Napoli divertissement* for the Royal Ballet.

Guest Artist Belinda Wright with Christopher Gable

FLOWER FESTIVAL
AT GENZANO

Pas de deux

NAPOLI *Divertissement*   during performance

FAR LEFT Gary Sherwood
lifts Elizabeth Anderton,
flanked by Shirley Grahame,
and Brenda Last.
BELOW Maryon Lane,
Shirley Grahame, Brenda Last,
and Elizabeth Anderton

Anthony Dowell's excellent line and pliant technique invariably catch the eye, particularly in his *Napoli* variation.

In his first leading rôle as the Country Boy in Andrée Howard's haunting and wistful *La Fête Étrange*, Dowell also managed to sustain a sure dramatic quality matching the mood of the work. Any lack of the right atmosphere affects this beautiful ballet more disastrously than most. If it is to retain the quality of Alain-Fournier's novel (which provides the episode upon which the ballet is based), then the characterisation should not be remote and uninvolved as some critics seem to suggest. Everything should happen with the heightened sensitivity of a dream yet the central characters should in no way remain unsubstantial and remote; each must feel the other's presence deeply—as Anthony Dowell and Lynn Seymour can suggest when cast opposite each other in this ballet. The brief encounter has a lasting effect on the lives of both characters.

Rehearsing
NAPOLI

Anthony Dowell in his
variation, watched by
Antoinette Sibley,
Brian Shaw, and
Georgina Parkinson

Maryon Lane
and
Christopher
Gable
in
Napoli

BELOW Erik Bruhn, who mounted
Napoli and the *Flower Festival*
pas de deux for the Royal Ballet,
goes over a movement from the
pas de deux for the benefit of
Shirley Grahame and Laurence Ruffell
while on tour in Greece. Rudolf
Nureyev, who danced the male rôle
in America (once standing in at short
notice for Bruhn), adds
a suggestion of his own.

Kenneth MacMillan's ballets inform us, to a greater or lesser extent, about individual human conditions; they flicker and convolute with an elaborate embroidery that gives a deceptive cover to the emotions drifting just beneath the rich surface. They probe and they pry; they lift things momentarily into the light, then let them sink back into their surroundings. They comment, but they never pass judgement.

They remind me of an overgrown pond on a still day. A bright light limns the calm surface, which is broken by familiar yet exotic plants. There are no real shadows; the very brightness is a warning. Each object seems so clearly defined, yet the more one looks the more one sees through the glittering surface, to the dark inverted reflection and beyond into the softly blurred depths, alive and uneasy. His range is wide and free-wheeling. A random selection from his works show such lovingly shaped microcosms as the sublime *Solitaire*; sombre sociology in *The Burrow*, smoothly tailored exercises with classical lineage such as *Le Baiser de la Fée*; to the tightly coiled expressionism of *The Rite of Spring*, the mathematical expositions of *Diversions*, straying onwards to the ambitious (but perhaps not fully resolved) essay *Symphony*, set to Shostakovich's No. 1 Symphony. There is also the fairy-tale mysteriousness of *House of Birds* with its allegorical undertones, the crucially arresting theatrical drama of *The Invitation* and the brightly enjoyable charades of *La Création du Monde*.

It is a large palette which MacMillan uses, and he is constantly at work blending his pigments in new exercises, with a variety and effect which leave us constantly guessing as to which path he will next invite us to explore.

The revised production of *House of Birds* gave MacMillan the chance to reburnish an early success from the days of Sadler's Wells Theatre Ballet. He was fortunate in having Maryon Lane, who created the part of The Girl in the original production, available for the new production as well, and she was able to employ her immense artistry and feeling to the full. With Christopher Gable cast as The Boy, MacMillan felt safe in reworking the final stages of the ballet and giving equal weight to the male lead; he thus used Gable's facility as the foundation for a new and sparkling *divertissement* to act as a finale, and the whole ballet came up fresh and exciting. The Georgiadis settings were revised by the artist and looked glowing and powerful, and the music by Federico Mompou remained an undeniable asset. The haunting piano pieces cast their spell from the first note. I don't think I missed a single rehearsal of 'Birds.' The music was like a drug and I could never hear enough of it. Seeing the choreography tailored to it so perfectly was equally rewarding, and the leading dancers interpreted their rôles to perfection.

Kenneth MacMillan
at a rehearsal of
House of Birds

HOUSE
of
BIRDS

Kenneth MacMillan begins
rehearsing the revival of his
ballet with the principals
Christopher Gable and Maryon
Lane as The Boy and The Girl

MacMillan's shapes have a deep backbone of classicism with often only the barest of variants accentuating his personal theme. A hand or head angle provides a subtle yet definite accent; in this instance, The Girl's backward thrust of the head balances perfectly the forward droop of her left hand.

The entrance of The Boy and The Girl who have strayed, unawares, near the house of the evil Bird Woman, who sells her enchanted victims to sinister merchants

The Girl turns inwards and folds slowly under The Boy's arm, ending up in a fully supported pose (ABOVE).

What are seemingly the simplest of movements demand just that extra degree of dexterity. LEFT Gable's right forearm has had to do a backward twist of a full 180 degrees from the elbow, in order to accommodate the ensuing turn by Maryon Lane

RIGHT A glimpse forward, to the completed move as it ultimately appears on stage

Elizabeth Anderton as The Girl,
with Christopher Gable

The Girl and The Boy begin a carefree dance, in tight
square floor patterns with the partners changing dextrously
from corner to corner in semi-jive idiom, never separated
by more than the length of an arm. In these swift
interchanges of position, the arm and body lines
retain an echo of the boxed floor pattern. The final
shoulder lift keeps to the angular, interlocking design.

These pictures illustrate that despite the speed and
complexity of positions in the choreography, there need
never be any sense of physical strain or lack of sympathy
between the dancers. The relaxed hands are a telling feature.

MacMillan's fizzy choreography nevertheless sets a tiring pace

Conductor Ashley Lawrence's
sensitive reading of the Mompou
score was one of the factors
contributing towards the success
of the ballet, and he maintained
a vital sympathy with the dancers'
interpretive moods

The Boy, dismayed by The Girl's physical transformation (under the spell of The Bird Woman), reaches forward questioningly; the movement of this natural instinct is still in harmony with the established pattern of line

Kenneth MacMillan demonstrates a position
he requires from the dancers. Whether he
is creating a new ballet or making a revision
(as in this instance), MacMillan has the
firmest idea of what he wants, long before
he commences working with his raw material.
This is not to say that he does not absorb
the personalities of his leading dancers
to a remarkable degree—he draws from
them constantly.

LEFT The Boy retains his 'human' line;
The Girl has become 'bird.' Together, they
form a neatly interlocking apex design

141

The moments when The Boy
and The Girl are together, before
the latter is enticed away by
The Bird Woman as The Boy
lies sleeping

Once inside the house,
The Girl is snared by her captor.
Shirley Grahame plays the part
of the ageless Bird Woman

Alarmed by The Girl's disappearance, The Boy breaks
into the House of Birds. He sees The Girl, but his
relief soon turns to torment; his despairing embraces
cannot rouse her. Though her mind is unchanged,
she is unable to respond to him with her now strangely
inarticulate body

Lane and Gable

Wells and Gable

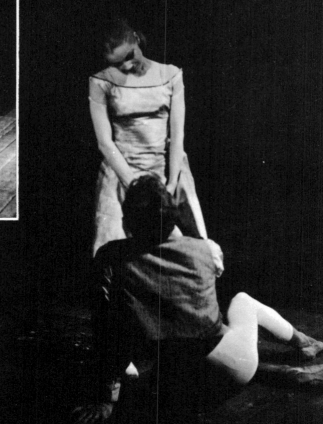

During performance

146

Lane and Gable

Lane and Gable

ABOVE The Boy and The Girl together, shortly before the latter is enticed away from The Boy's side by The Bird Woman, who shows The Girl a vision of the gaily coloured birds fluttering inside her house. The Girl barely hesitates before deciding it is safe to leave The Boy sleeping, while she enters the House.

The ingenious costumes of the 'birds' created considerable effect, particularly the enchanted girls' wings (activated by arms flapped while akimbo), which set up an ominous and strangely authentic clattering. The whole ballet fascinated the contingent of Bolshoi dancers watching the last-of-the-season performance of *House of Birds*. They sought out the principals, flapped their arms in spirited fashion to intimate the ballet they were discussing, and chorused 'Good; good!'

The evil Bird Woman with her legion she has recruited by transforming boys

Inside the House, The Girl is fascinated
by the exotic birds. She is encouraged
to feed them. Slowly, The Bird Woman
exerts her malevolent influence and in a
chilling sequence we see The Girl flutter
and jerk into strange avian movements.
Finally, the transformation is total.
The new bird is snared by The Bird Woman
and darts helplessly at the end of a
restraining cord

Doreen Wells
in performance

Wells and Gable in performance

Having broken into the House, The Boy tries to grasp The Girl in her demented flight. In a blind rage, he struggles to release all the caged birds

Set free of their restraining cages the birds turn against their captor,
swooping and diving with menacing intent as the confused Bird Woman strives
desperately to avoid their attacks. The Boy pursues her, finally pinioning
her while the birds peck her to death. With her end, the spell is broken

Lane
and
Gable

154

The Boy and The Girl, free once more, dance together—an evocation of their opening *pas de deux*, now in more abandoned and exultant mood.

The liberated boys and girls join them. The girls momentarily prevent The Girl from joining The Boy. They do a very poignant dance together, with soft rhythmical arm movements in contrast to their earlier frenetic bird-like fluttering

Wells and Gable
during performance

Lane and Gable

Ronald Emblen

Michael Coleman

In the final *divertissement* by the released boys and girls,
there is a breezy *pas de trois* performed by three boys. They
whirl on to the stage one after the other, then follow a circular
pattern with a variety of *tours en l'air*. Interpolated into
this dance is a spirited variation for The Boy

The climax of the jubilant dance is an exciting (and fiendishly difficult) coda by The Boy. Urged on by staccato clapping from the others, he whirls diagonally across the stage; the tucking of the right foot on each *tour en l'air* giving the appearance of a pumping action reminiscent of a child's mechanical top. MacMillan here exploited Gable's technique with spectacular and novel effect, but the movement has been a trap for successors to the rôle.

The curtain falls as The Boy and The Girl are left alone together on the empty stage.

House of Birds
Concluded

Light-hearted Interlude

Annette Page's usually immaculate upswept
hair fought free of its restraining pins
during an exercise of *pirouettes*. Margot
Fonteyn stopped to enjoy the bizarre effect

LA SYLPHIDE

Margot Fonteyn in an extract from
Act II of the famous Danish version

165

The Highlander James (Rudolf Nureyev) has wrapped the beautiful and elusive Sylphide in the magic gossamer scarf. Unaware of the scarf's evil properties, he is aghast as the delicate creature falls dying

GAYANEH

Gayaneh

Although *Gayaneh* is not in the Royal Ballet repertoire, I cannot resist including these pictures of the *pas de deux*; the demure wit and style that Fonteyn brings to this tiny extract from the Soviet ballet is so perfect that every lilt and flicker becomes fixed irrevocably in the mind. Like her portrait of Chloë, its image seems

complete, untouchable, unalterable. Nureyev's bravura is the perfect foil, and what is more, the Fonteyn-Nureyev version seems to be full of inimitable Kurdish touches which appear to have been lost from such Soviet extracts as have been seen in the West.

LA BAYADÈRE

Margot Fonteyn and Rudolf Nureyev as Nikiya and Solor, in Nureyev's valuable and beautiful reproduction for the Royal Ballet of *The Kingdom of the Shades* Act from the historic ballet

Sitting idly in the sunshine which
slanted through the tall windows
of the classroom in the Nice Opera
House I felt a guilt, induced by
the activities of the class all
around, which finally made me pick
up my camera and turn it on the
nearest person—Ronald Hynd. His
marvellous mock expression of amazement
and affront was worth the effort!

RIGHT Annette Page (Mrs Hynd)
rehearsing the *pas de deux* from
Don Quixote, during the Athens Festival

Annette Page in the *Don Quixote pas de deux*
costume, photographed in the Herod Atticus
Theatre, Athens, where the dancer gave a
marvellously precise and stylish display before
a huge and wildly enthusiastic audience

SYMPHONIC VARIATIONS

Annette Page
in one of the
signature poses
from the Ashton
ballet set to
César Franck's
music

A sonnet, a dream; all
purity and revelation. It runs
like a mountain stream and flowers
with the simplicity of a white
lily. If only one could capture even
a thread of its harmony as it unravels.

There is a quintessence of England
about it. Greeks appreciate it, yet
it could never be Greek. Impossibly
beautiful, it is Ashton's rarest jewel

Symphonic Variations at dawn in the Herod Atticus Theatre, with the Acropolis somewhere high above; the *only* setting for which I would trade Sophie Fedorovitch's perfect backcloth —Shirley Grahame, Margot Fonteyn, Annette Page, and Alexander Grant

Georgina Parkinson

Having spent so much time there between rehearsals, I feel honour
bound to make some passing acknowledgement of the canteen at the Royal
Ballet School at Hammersmith. Its utilitarian setting is as familiar
to the Company as the Opera House stage, and provides the background
for these two random, informal portraits taken after work

176

Donald Britton in TOCCATA

Alan Carter's ballet is one of those 'this is us all informal, dancing together between rehearsals just for the joy of it' sort of pieces. It always needs a naïve audience to swallow *that* premise, and not surprisingly, the critics made some terse remarks about it, but given with the Touring Section's infectious whole-heartedness it is a painless enough confection. Nobody can complain about the music.

Donald Britton usually finds room for comedy and swagger in the 'period' solo.

THE RITE OF SPRING

A milestone in the history of music, Stravinsky's score has provoked recurring milestones in the history of ballet. Its fierce, rhythmical complexity first tempted Nijinsky, and successive choreographers have found the music a demanding siren. Ritual sacrifice is its theme, as exhausted dancers are only too aware by the time the curtain falls. Kenneth MacMillan's version has a décor by Sidney Nolan, which includes plain flat expanses of fascinating brush work suggesting nascent brown earth. In Part Two, there is painted against a dark cobalt sky a huge disc-topped 'symbol,' golden and glittering like hewn quartz, which slowly turns blood-red. The girls all wear long, flaxen-white hair, while the boys sport dark top-knots.

Monica Mason as the Chosen Maiden

*Ninette
de Valois
rehearsing
her ballet*

THE
RAKE'S
PROGRESS

ABOVE Dame Ninette in full cry, flanked by Ailne Phillips and Michael Somes

LEFT With Kenneth Mason

Alexander Grant as The Rake,
with Leslie Edwards as The Bravo

'Madam' required an effect of cowering. She got it!

THE RAKE'S PROGRESS

*The
Dancing
Lesson*

Alexander Grant and Brian Shaw

Alexander Grant
and
Brian Shaw

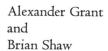

The entrance of the
betrayed Girl. Julie Wood
as The Mother and
Antoinette Sibley as
The Girl

A delightful cameo
from Keith Martin,
in the guise of the
scruffy Jockey

BELOW Gerd Larsen as
The Dancer, with Robert
Mead as The Rake's Friend

RIGHT The Girl
offers her savings to
the Creditors who
press The Rake

Antoinette Sibley
David Drew
Leslie Edwards
Franklin White
Alexander Grant

Antoinette Sibley in front of the famous Rex Whistler drop-cloth

Alexander Grant

Antoinette Sibley   Robert Mead

Kenneth Mason as
The Gentleman with the Rope

In the Lunatic Asylum

Robert Mead as The Card Player

The death of
The Rake
(at rehearsal—
consequently
with hair!)

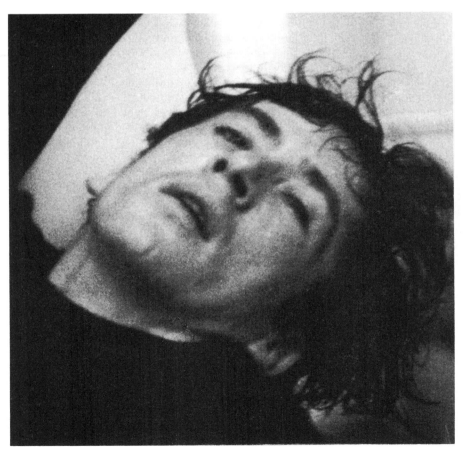

Anya Linden
as The Wife in
THE INVITATION

I am not certain that ballet photographs posed out of doors have any real validity, any more than those usual publicity photos, with ersatz slices of action taking place on huge rolls of paper in the photographer's studio, but with the discovery of one particularly atmospheric setting I was anxious to experiment. Fortunately, Anya Linden and Desmond Doyle, who give such memorable portrayal as The Man and Wife in *The Invitation*, fell in with my whims. We let the setting provide the mood for moments from the ballet. It was an interesting afternoon. Two children playing in the surroundings saw absolutely nothing unusual about the activity of the couple in the garden, but perhaps their memories will contain some curious, dreamlike images in future years?

The setting for the ballet itself is a Colonial home in South America at the turn of the century, brilliantly evoked by Georgiadis' arborescent sets.

Anya Linden and Desmond Doyle

THE INVITATION

(The following forty-three photographs were taken during the course of one dress rehearsal)

The Mother (Gerd Larsen) after primly restraining the mild curiosity of two visiting children towards naked statuary in her garden, provides modesty drapes for the offending figures before her garden-party begins

Her daughter (Lynn Seymour) appears in the garden, followed closely by the girl's young cousin (Christopher Gable), who is staying on the estate

His somewhat gauche displays of budding tenderness towards her are soon rudely interrupted by the arrival of other children

Smart and curious, one of the boys has dragged away
the statues' new drapery. The children are momentarily
intrigued by the uncompromising figures but quickly
lose interest after a session of boisterous teasing,
which is eventually broken up by the The Boy's suddenly
protective attitude towards The Girl's feelings

The guests' arrival brings the children to order. The Boy is still awkward and unsure, and a shade remorseful about his earlier complicity in the teasing of the Girl; they are locked in their own uneasy rapport as The Wife arrives and turns to wait for her husband (LEFT). With his arrival, a sense of strain between the couple is at once apparent. The man's eyes rest on the young daughter of the house, and he advances towards her with elaborate, intent courtesy. The Wife puts a restraining hand on his shoulder (LOWER LEFT) then she advances, and with a display of calculated charm, allows the impressed Boy to take her hand. At this moment The Husband moves forward (ABOVE) and deliberately brushes aside the youth's gesture

Later, the two young cousins witness The Man and Wife locked in a violent quarrel

OVERLEAF The first statue has been uncovered, and the confused Girl has been forced to view it squarely by her cousin

The younger couple are left alone. There is a brief dance, with The Girl displaying a new sympathy towards The Boy. She is by turns tender and puckish, and faintly puzzled by her own swiftly changing emotions. She avoids the boy's attempts to kiss her, but finally adds to his bafflement by giving *him* a noisy, impulsive kiss before darting away

In a large, empty room of the mansion, The Man and Wife continue their antagonistic duet. The Wife is edgily neurotic in behaviour, while he is sternly unsympathetic towards her alternate fits of pleading and bitterness. He is exasperated; in no mood to make any concessions or accept conciliatory moves from her. He rejects her angrily, and goaded to a point of physical roughness, finally flings the unhappy woman from him, leaving her ashamed and humiliated.

The room is suddenly filled with the children, due to receive a dancing lesson from a tyrannical governess. From the side, The Man and Wife regain their composure and stay to watch the activity among the younger people. The Man finds himself unaccountably aware of the Young Girl, while The Boy is innocently happy that the woman whose adult beauty so recently astonished him, should display a warmth towards him. Encouraged by the competitive nature of the lesson, and unwittingly susceptible to the hint of more sophisticated competition, The Girl impulsively sets herself at the older man. She dances towards him with a youthful, almost voluptuous abandonment. With cool deliberation, he steps forward, and begins to accompany her. They commence slowly, The Man guiding The Girl with subtle assuredness. She responds to the partnering and the dance gradually develops in intensity. Both The Man and The Girl are oblivious to the fact that the others are standing still watching; mystified, curious, and perhaps a little frightened. The Governess, fiercely mesmerised, does nothing. At the height of the display, The Girl's mother arrives in the room; she is astonished at what she sees. The uneasy Wife unconvincingly attempts to persuade her hostess that there is nothing untoward in the Husband's behaviour, but the dance is brought to an abrupt conclusion.

During this uneasy display, the reorientation of awareness and disturbing intuitiveness can be seen written on the face of The Boy (*i.e.*, the face of Christopher Gable in the lower photograph), more clearly than any pages of words could elaborate upon

The evening moves towards its dark and seemingly inevitable
climax. The Wife misses the opportunity to speak with The
Girl, whom she sees running in the darkened garden which is alive with restless, predatory
couples and bizarrely costumed entertainers. Drained by emotional conflict, tormented, The Wife
suddenly surrenders to the physical attractiveness of
the unsure Boy. She *allows* herself—almost
passively—to seduce him

Seduction is too gentle a word for events elsewhere in the tangled garden. The Girl's questioning, tender moves towards The Man trigger a violent and terrible course of action from him. She is helpless and she is brutally violated

Swiftly overcome with horror at the outrage
he has just committed, The Man flees,
leaving The Girl in a shocked, voiceless agony

Staggering separate ways in the garden, they collide again. The Man reaches towards The Girl with a desperate and beseeching gesture, but she recoils from him in terror and he sinks helplessly to his knees. His wife appears, shattered with remorse and fear. Confronted with the evidence, she kneels by her husband and slowly takes his arm. There can be no reproach, only a strong effort of will to withdraw from the immediate situation—together

The Boy enters. The Girl, broken, in a state of shock, and desperately in need of comfort, rushes to him. With relief and compassion he clasps her tightly and then kisses her. The effect is catastrophic. The Girl backs away from him in uncontrollable loathing. He turns and runs blindly into the comforting darkness, leaving her struggling to master an astringent dignity that may possibly propel her through the long, frigid torment of her future life.

Lynn Seymour and Christopher Gable won wide acclaim for their creations of the young cousins when the ballet was first seen in December 1960. All the tentativeness, impetuousity, and vulnerability of adolescence was suggested with the most subtle nuances, yet, like all truly great interpretive artists, they continue to strike even closer to the quintessence of youth in these rôles, though they themselves grow older. Today, their performances remain astonishing and profound theatre.

COPPÉLIA

Coppélia had been out of the repertory some considerable time before it returned in the autumn of 1963. Despite its persistently aggravating plot and arbitrary development as a ballet, the production gave many people a pleasant surprise with its air of freshness and attack. As a vehicle for Swanilda, it demands tremendous soubrette qualities to sustain the key rôle. The tiresome Franz, with his spasmodic bursts of activity, is for this very reason a difficult and ungrateful part for male dancers. Only the most powerful dramatic personalities make any real impression in this department.

Leslie Edwards takes a rehearsal with three casts for the rôle of Franz: Christopher Gable, Graham Usher, and Kenneth Mason

John Hart, Assistant Director to the Company, rehearsing Kenneth Mason in the butterfly sequence prior to Mason's début as Franz at Covent Garden. With him as Swanilda is Maryon Lane, one of the really notable Swanildas of recent years

Not surprisingly, the Royal Ballet's most interesting Franz proved to be Gable, who teamed with Antoinette Sibley for the opening night which thus had a sparkling pair to re-launch the production.

The butterfly sequence is one of *Coppélia's* time-honoured sequences of mime which can still manage to look fresh if acted with complete conviction.

Swanilda has been chasing a butterfly. Franz helps her catch it.

After examining its beauty, the thoughtless Franz takes a pin from his lapel and stabs the creature, using it as a decoration for his waistcoat. Swanilda is dismayed by the callous act

The same moment as it appears on stage

'But what's the matter? It's only a butterfly . . .'
Swanilda turns away in distress

ABOVE Antoinette Sibley rehearsing
the 'ear of corn' episode. Swanilda
is told that the ear of corn will
make music when shaken—only so
long as her swain is faithful to
her. She shakes it, but is dismayed when her friends claim they
can hear no response. Franz has
been flirting with the old toymaker's lifelike doll, Coppélia,
which sits in a window above the
town square

Franz and Swanilda
commence the *pas de deux*
from Act I

RIGHT Although this position is only the briefest moment of pause during action, I find its harmony and counterpoint of line extraordinarily satisfying. One can continue to discover wonderful mathematical ratios the more one studies the grouping

Antoinette Sibley talks to
Conductor Emanuel Young

220

The *pas de deux*
from Act III

ACT II

In Dr Coppélius' workshop.
Seeking Coppélia, Franz has climbed
in at a window. He creeps forward
into the dark, sinister room.
Coppélius is in the shadows,
tailing him.

ABOVE Two casts for Dr Coppélius:
Franklin White and Stanley Holden

Each time Franz turns around, Coppélius freezes, pretending to be another doll

BELOW Double casts at work. In relief, Franz points to the figure of Coppélius. 'Why, it's only another doll after all!'

Stanley Holden as Coppélius, with Christopher Gable . . .

Franz turns away again and is immediately seized by the ear. The irate Coppélius chases Franz around the workshop

. . . and with Graham Usher

Unable to escape, Franz faces the old toymaker. 'I think you're an old devil!'

Having assured Coppélius that he had no intention of stealing from the workshop, Franz mimes to the effect that they should both be friends. After all, Coppélius is the guardian of the beautiful Coppélia. 'Fine!' says Coppélius. 'Have a drink to seal our friendship.' The wily old man has slipped a drug into the bottle

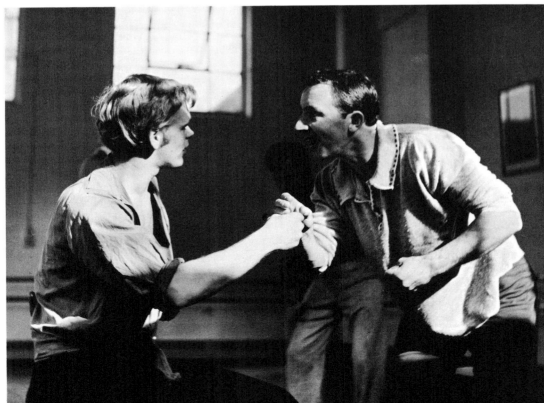

The drug takes effect (RIGHT).
Swanilda, who has already concealed
herself in Coppélius' cupboard
and taken the place of the doll
Coppélia, rushes to Franz while
the Doctor's back is turned. It
is no use; Franz is destined
to spend the rest of Act II asleep
at the table

So much of this book is an obvious tribute to the choreography of Sir Frederick Ashton that there is perhaps little point in making the last section a *specific* homage to his art, but I want to try to record some of the harmonies and invention of line which proliferate through his *pas de deux* work in particular. For this purpose, I have chosen the glorious double work in Ashton's *La Fille mal Gardée*, the first full-length English ballet to be labelled an unqualified and undoubted *classic* in the strictest sense of the word.

That wonderfully exhilarating performance given at the end of the 1963 summer season in London was watched by a large contingent from the Bolshoi, and it earned the ballet a deserved accolade: the Russians asked the choreographer if he would be prepared to mount the ballet for them.

Before I take a closer look at *La Fille mal Gardée*, it seems worth remembering that one of Frederick Ashton's earliest ballets for the original company was the simple and sparkling *Les Rendezvous*, set to bouncy music by Auber. First seen in December 1933 it is, happily, still in the repertory. Its inconsequential theme of boys and girls meeting in a park is the thread for a delightfully constructed work, full of exuberance and zest with strong lateral and diagonal patterns; the leading male dancer zooms across the stage in spirited strides (LOWER RIGHT), and numerous travelling lifts in and out of the wings are performed *en masse* by all the partners. The first cast in 1933 included Markova, de Valois, and Helpmann. In the first of many new productions (November 16, 1937) the cast contained Fonteyn, Ashton himself, and Jill Gregory—now Ballet Mistress.

Les Rendezvous, like *Les Patineurs*, goes into that rare box marked Indestructible.

LES
RENDEZVOUS

Christopher Gable

Annette Page

Maryon Lane

Nadia Nerina

Choreographic sequences from

Ashton's

LA FILLE MAL GARDÉE

Act I, Scene I

Lise and Colas are in the habit of leaving lovers' messages for one another in the form of silk ribbons placed at strategic spots in the farmyard of Lise's home. Early in the morning Lise emerges from the farm-house; her first move is to look if Colas has left her a ribbon. She even climbs the loft ladder in her search but can see no trace of a message. Colas has in fact not yet paid his morning call to the farm. After testing the bowl of cream from the dairy, Lise's

Merle Park

Doreen Wells

spirits rise. From its hiding place in her bodice she takes a ribbon and happily begins to dance with it, describing numerous pretty shapes in the air as she does so.

Lise ends her dance. She looks for a suitable place to leave the new ribbon, finally deciding on a hitching ring in the barn wall. She ties the ribbon in a lover's bow, kisses it softly and then departs.

Colas enters the farmyard. He glances about for his ribbon, but at first cannot see it. He too tastes the bowl of cream (finding it much to his liking) and is then on the point of leaving, somewhat despondently, when he sights Lise's ribbon. He runs and plucks it from the wall, tying it with a flourish to the end of his stave. With broad, *demi-caractère* strides (RIGHT) he advances to the centre of the farmyard and begins an exhilarating solo consisting of many difficult turns and beats (the more difficult for having to hold the stave at both ends throughout), ending in a *grande pirouette à la seconde*.

Colas mounts the farm-house steps to
look for Lise, but is surprised
by the sudden appearance of the angry
Widow Simone. Colas survives a fusillade of
cabbages and pot-plants, manages to give
Lise a hasty greeting, then retreats before the
threatening Widow. Lise tries to
restore her mother's humour.

With the Widow's back turned momentarily, Colas reappears and endeavours
to entice Lise out of the farmyard
(ABOVE). While the Widow stumps off
to get the butter churn to keep Lise
occupied, there is a brief moment for
the lovers—during which Colas lifts
Lise with a fine one-handed *pressage*
(RIGHT), before the Widow returns.
Colas blows Lise a hasty kiss and then
departs.

Stanley Holden as the Widow, with Nadia Nerina (LEFT) and Merle Park (BELOW)

Lise, happy but flustered, hides the departing Colas from her mother's view. The Widow has no time for these antics. She makes Lise apply her energies to the churn, and she demonstrates with a few vigorous plunges of the handle

Her demonstrative zeal rocks the
heavy churn onto her own toe, with
agonising results. Hobbling with pain,
the Widow is forced to retire to the
farm-house. Lise is left to get on
with the churning

235

Nadia Nerina
and
David Blair

Colas takes the opportunity to re-emerge but his amorous entreaties cannot tempt the dutiful Lise from the churn. Seeing that he intends to leave, Lise relents, and plucking the ribbon from his stave, she begins a flirtatious game. She presses the ribbon to Colas, who shows that it should not be pressed to his right side but to his left—over his heart. Lise decides that his hands should be tied in that position. When Colas tries to kiss her, she darts back to the churn.

Merle Park and
Christopher Gable

Colas shows Lise that he is unable to
help her with the churning because his
hands are tied. Lise relents and unties
him, but after the briefest show of
energy Colas drifts to a halt (RIGHT).

Lise jumps up. Colas almost falls
off the bench, but in doing so he sees
another length of rolled ribbon which
has been left there.

Maryon Lane and Christopher Gable
during performance

Nadia Nerina and David Blair

Colas tosses the ribbon in a great arc
to Lise (LEFT), then winds himself rapidly
towards her. He kisses her lightly then
unwinds again, before Lise repeats
the action (LOWER SEQUENCE LEFT).

With the couple at both ends of the
ribbon once more, Lise gives her end to
Colas and remains inside the loop (TOP).
She runs around him and folds into his
arms with a *pirouette* and a lunge (ABOVE).

Maryon Lane and
Christopher Gable
during a rehearsal pause

Lise then runs downstage and begins a series of small *jetés*; at the height of each she is jerked backwards through the air by Colas (TOP LEFT), who then takes his turn in the harness (TOP RIGHT). Finally he puts the reins between his teeth (ABOVE) and mimes a spirited, high-stepping carriage horse, while Lise crosses the ribbons behind her back and urges him on with playful slaps from the loose ends. They drift to a halt. The musical score says at this point 'And love overtakes them . . .'

Lise *bourrées* inwards towards Colas and giving
the ribbon ends to him, turns in a suspended *attitude*

Colas also crosses the ribbons behind himself, then knots the two ends together. Each places one loop over the other's head, then they tuck their arms through the lower strands and duck together, emerging with a perfect cat's cradle which they proudly display

Maryon Lane and Christopher Gable
photographed on the stage of the Opera
House, immediately before the curtain
went up on a performance of *La Fille mal Gardée*
which captivated a full house at the Garden

Colas unties the ribbon, Lise runs back with one end, then Colas kneels and sets in motion a ripple like a sound wave

Lise *bourrées* down towards Colas with a series of *pas de chat* on point, jumping in and out of the ribbon. She does an *arabesque*, kisses Colas, and then retreats down the line of ribbon

This charming and decorative sequence
invariably draws very audible gasps of delight from the audience

Lise takes her end of
the ribbon again and
chaînés back to Colas,
who lifts her above
him. He turns her as
he retreats upstage,
slowly gathering speed.
Finally he lowers her
in a sweeping arc and
swoops her diagonally
across the stage.
Lise finishes on point with
a *port de bras* flourish
of the ribbon

The game is broken up by the arrival of Lise's friends. Attempting to depart with them, Lise is caught by the Widow, who is about to administer a sound spanking to her daughter when the rich Farmer Thomas and his simple-minded son Alain appear in the yard with gifts for the Widow and her daughter. Widow Simone hastily checks her action, converting it to a gay wave (RIGHT) and the quick smoothing down of Lise's skirts.

Lise and her mother go to change before the whole assembly departs for a picnic beside the harvested cornfield. There, Colas is the first of the party to arrive, and he produces bottles of wine for the thirsty harvesters (BELOW).

ABOVE The Royal Ballet's original Alain, Alexander Grant, in the picnic *pas de trois*
BELOW Alan Alder as Alain

In Scene II, Lise is encouraged to dance with the witless (but wealthy) Alain, while Colas dodges about, concealing himself from the farmer's son. Somehow Colas always manages to emerge in the happiest position during this hilarious *pas de trois*

Alain is unaware that it is anything more than a normal *pas de deux*. With studiousness he matches, and even outshines, Lise's *arabesque*—with his arm!

Merle Park,
Christopher Gable,
and Alexander Grant

While the Widow and Farmer Thomas are inspecting the cornfield and discussing their proposed match between Lise and Alain, there is the time for the great *pas de deux* of Scene II. It is known in the Company as the Fanny Elssler *Pas de Deux*, being set to a piece of music which the famous dancer invariably inserted into her rôles as particularly suitable for a display of her technical prowess. While remaining very light and gay, the Ashton version also demands the greatest technical ability from both dancers.

The *pas de deux* begins with greetings between Lise and Colas in quick interchanges of position

Park and Gable (ABOVE)

Lane and Gable—
in performance (LEFT)

Lise's solo is marked by big travelling
jumps and variously phrased *attitudes* on point

Merle Park

Maryon Lane

She does a quick *arabesque penchée* towards
the watching Colas, during her solo

The choreographer keeps a check on his ballet. The above position comes from the ensuing ribbon dance, in which all Lise's friends join in

With their ribbons, the girls begin this cornfield dance by forming the rays of the sun. Lise
and Colas move in and out towards each other along the avenues of ribbons, before each takes four
ribbon ends from the girls. Colas *promenades* Lise on point, then takes a position downstage,
with Lise moving down to him between the ribbons. He eventually places her
in an *attitude* supported by all the ribbons, before moving away, leaving the girls to run
in a huge circle revolving Lise at the hub. Colas finally goes to support her again and lifts
her to his shoulder while she scatters the ribbons in a shower around them both.

They continue their *pas de deux*, with the girls marking changes in the music with elaborate ribbon patterns as a background. The *pas de deux* ends with Lise seated on Colas' knee, and the girls in an apex formation behind them releasing their ribbon design on the last note of music

Maryon Lane and Christopher Gable

MacMillan's

ROMEO
and
JULIET

with Christopher Gable
and Lynn Seymour
as Romeo and Juliet

". . . And palm to palm is holy palmers' kiss."

Show a fair presence and put on these frowns . . .

Despite Tybalt's ire at discovering Romeo in the
Capulet ballroom, Lord Capulet demands that the
young Montague remain and take the hand of a guest

Michael Somes as Capulet
Julia Farron as Lady Capulet
Desmond Doyle as Tybalt and
Gerd Larsen as The Nurse

Mercutio has been mortally wounded
by a thrust from Tybalt

David Blair as Mercutio, taking his
rapier for a last dying effort

Anthony Dowell as Benvolio

"Now, Tybalt, take the villain back again, . . ."
Romeo avenges his friend's death

Romeo: "This day's black fate on more days doth depend;
This but begins the woe others must end."

Urged on by the Capulets, Paris woes Juliet for her
consent to marriage. Already secretly married to
Romeo, Juliet is finally driven to the course of
desperation that is to end in double tragedy

Derek Rencher as Paris

LEFT Juliet: "O, sweet my mother, cast me not away!
Delay this marriage for a month, a week;"